My family photo

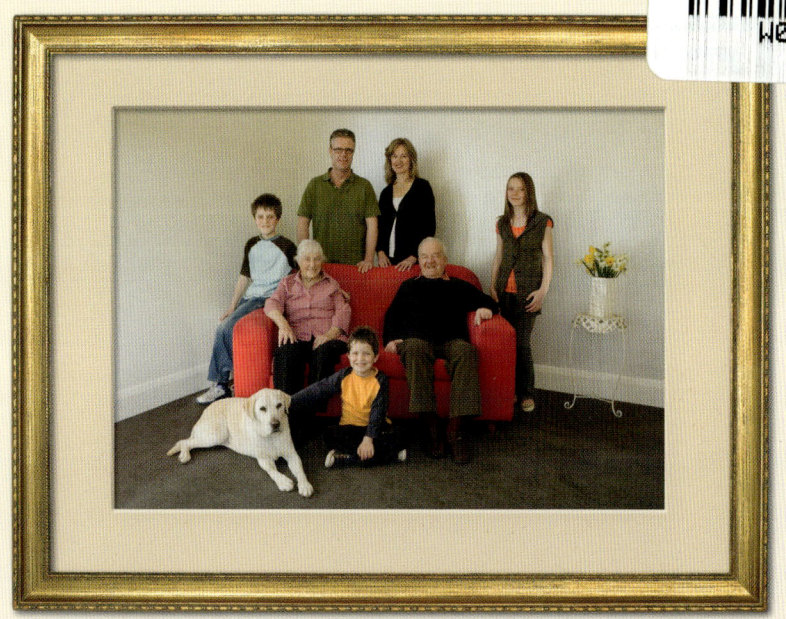

My dad is big.

He goes here.

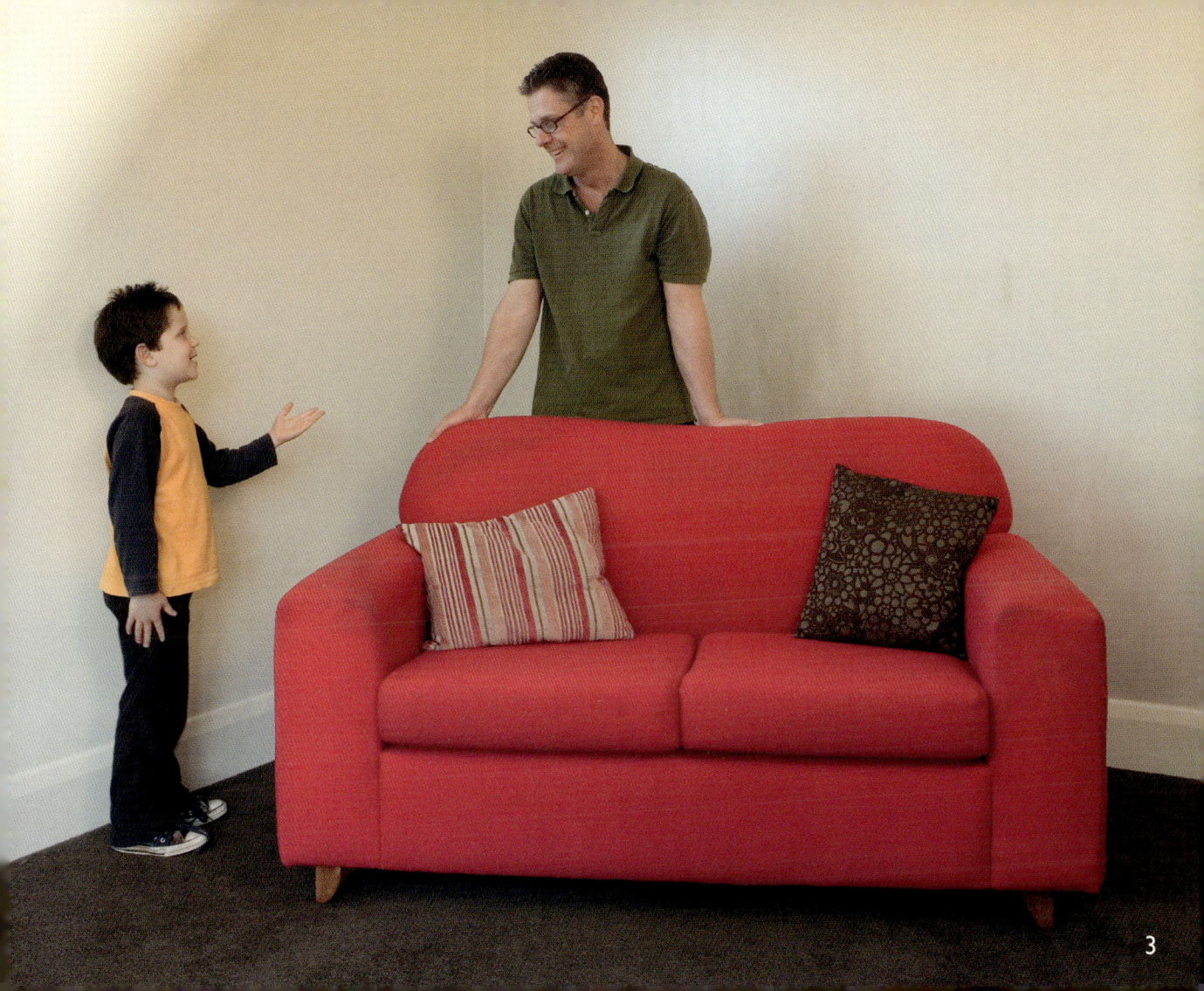

My mum is big.

She goes here.

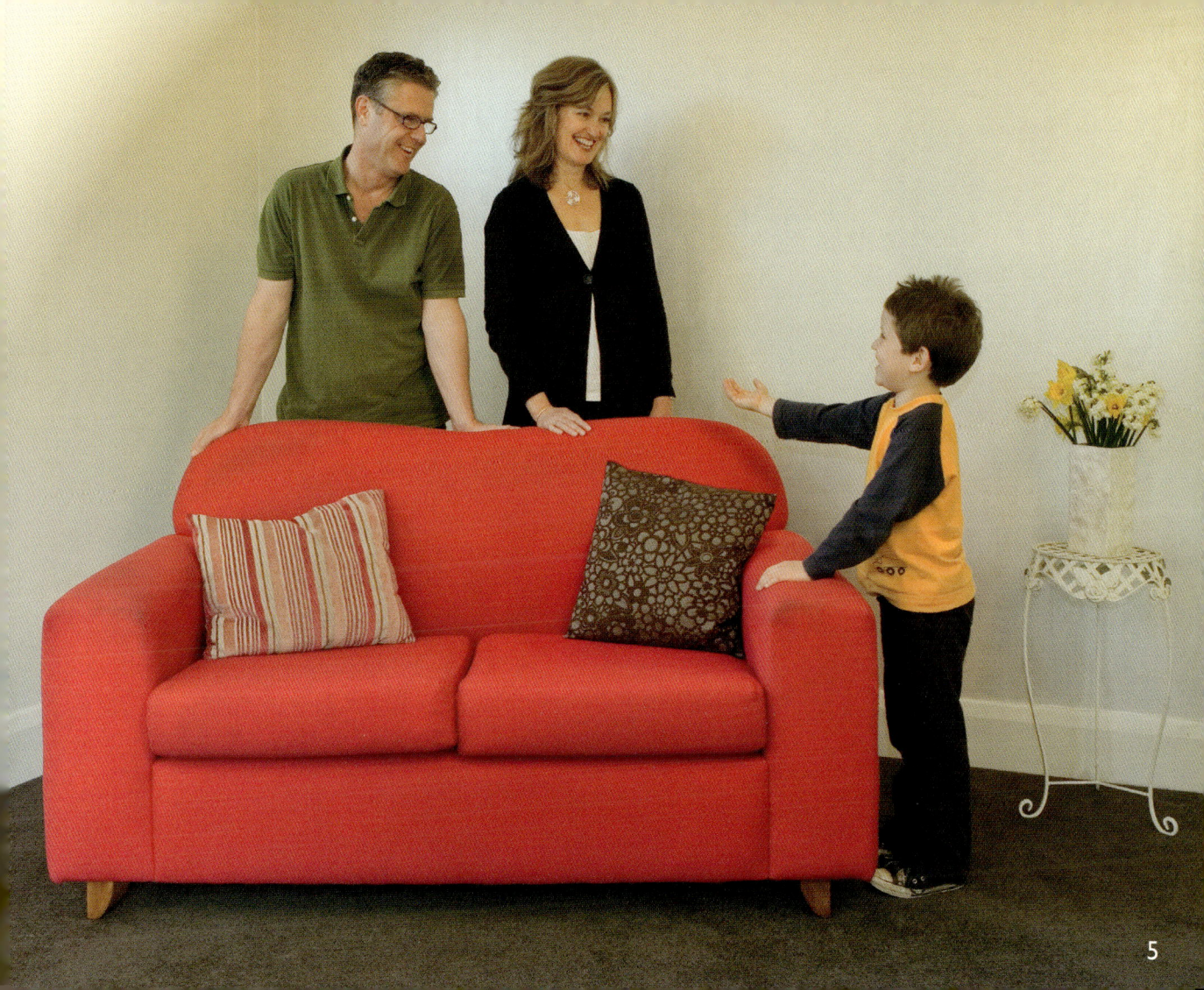

My grandpa is big.

He goes here.

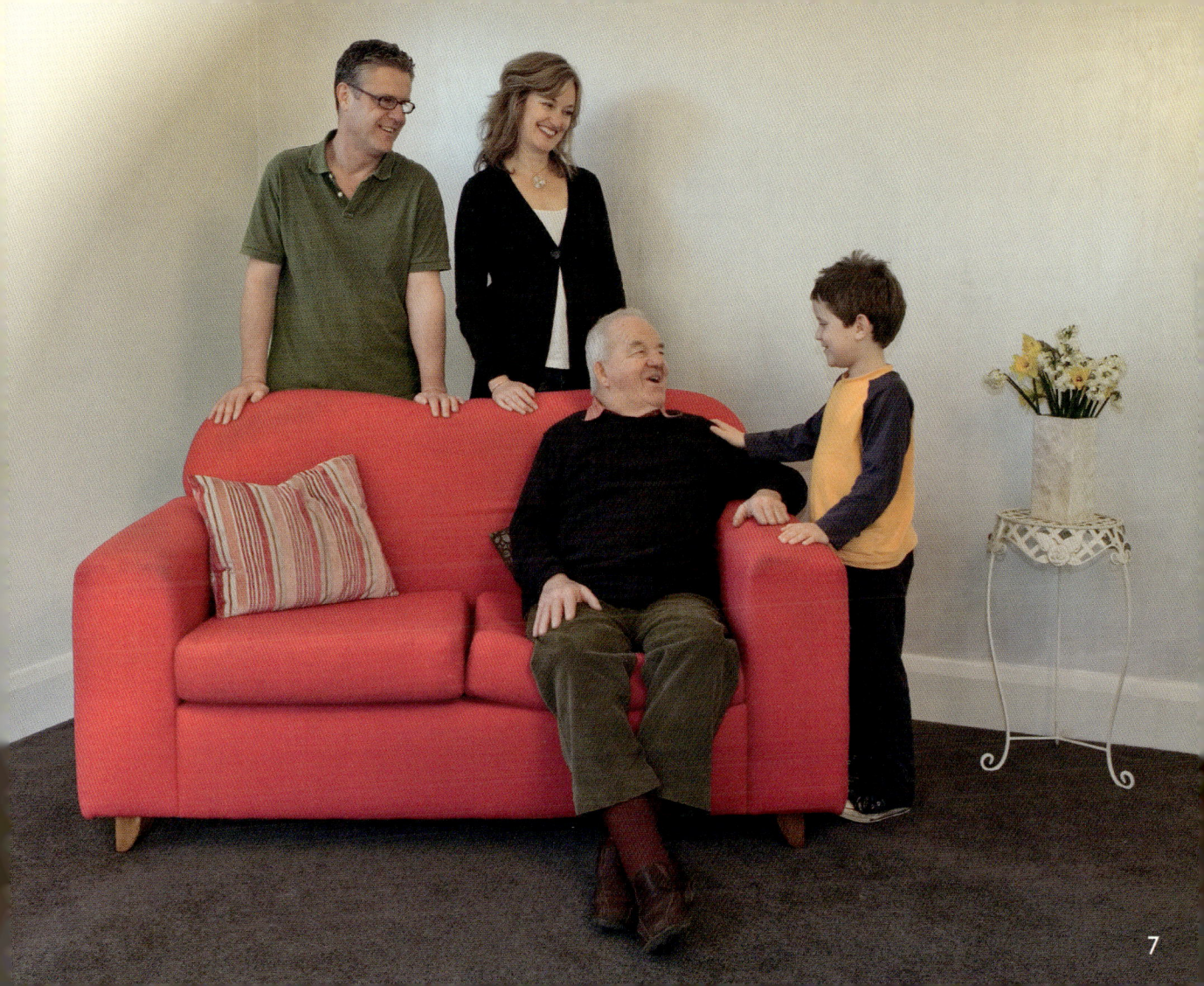

My grandma is big.

She goes here.

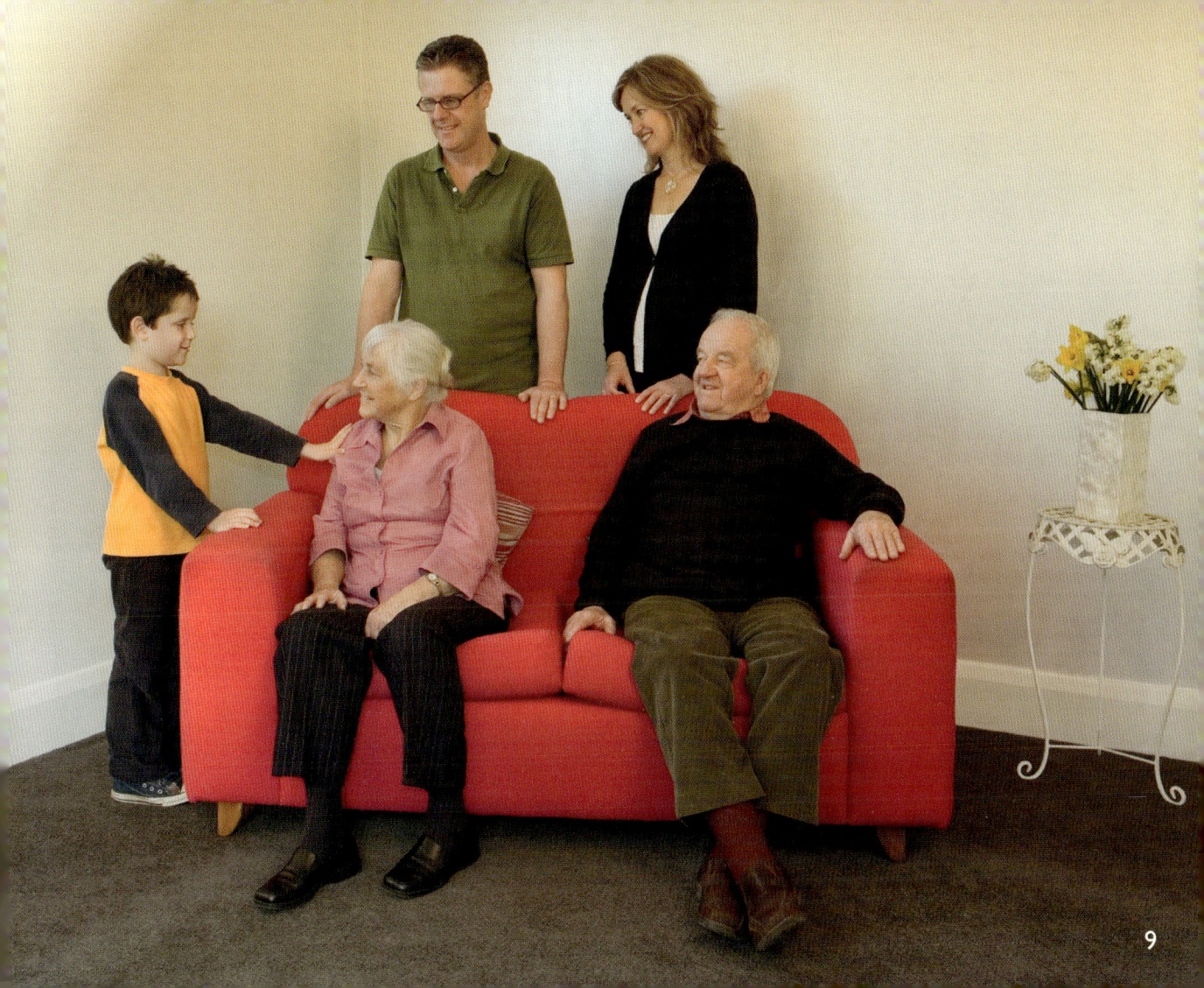

My sister is big.

She goes here.

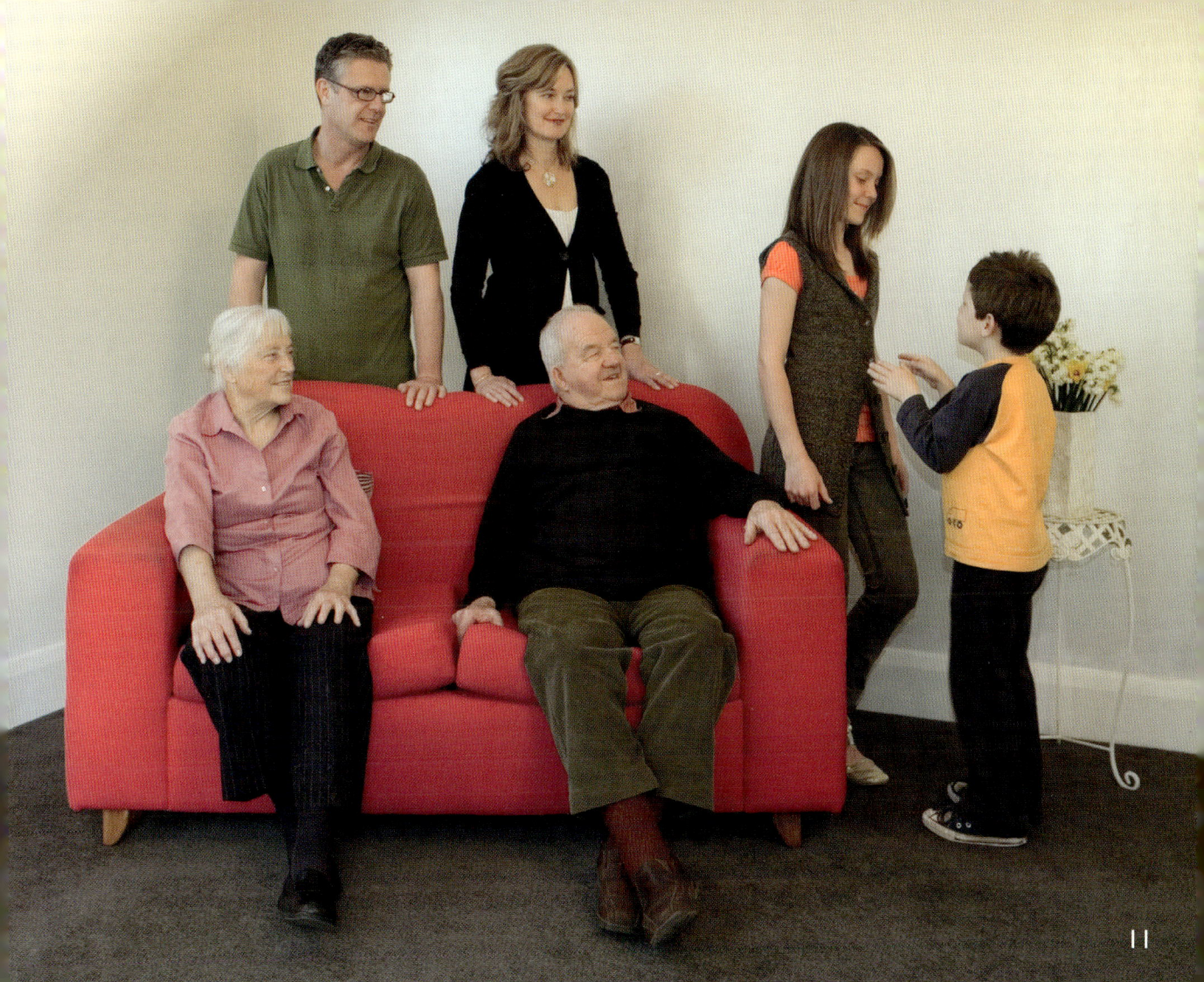

My brother is big.

He goes here.

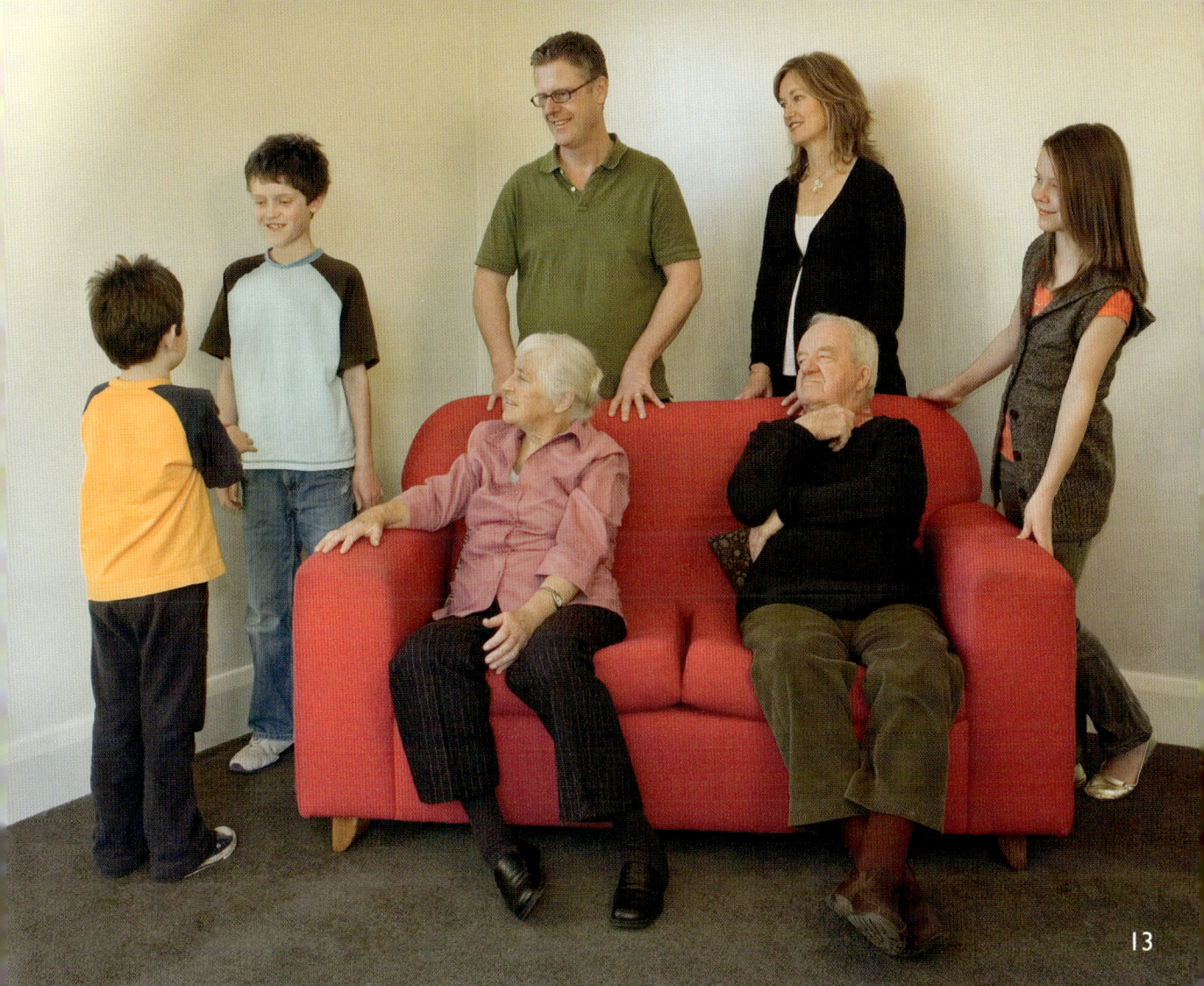

My dog is big.

She goes here.

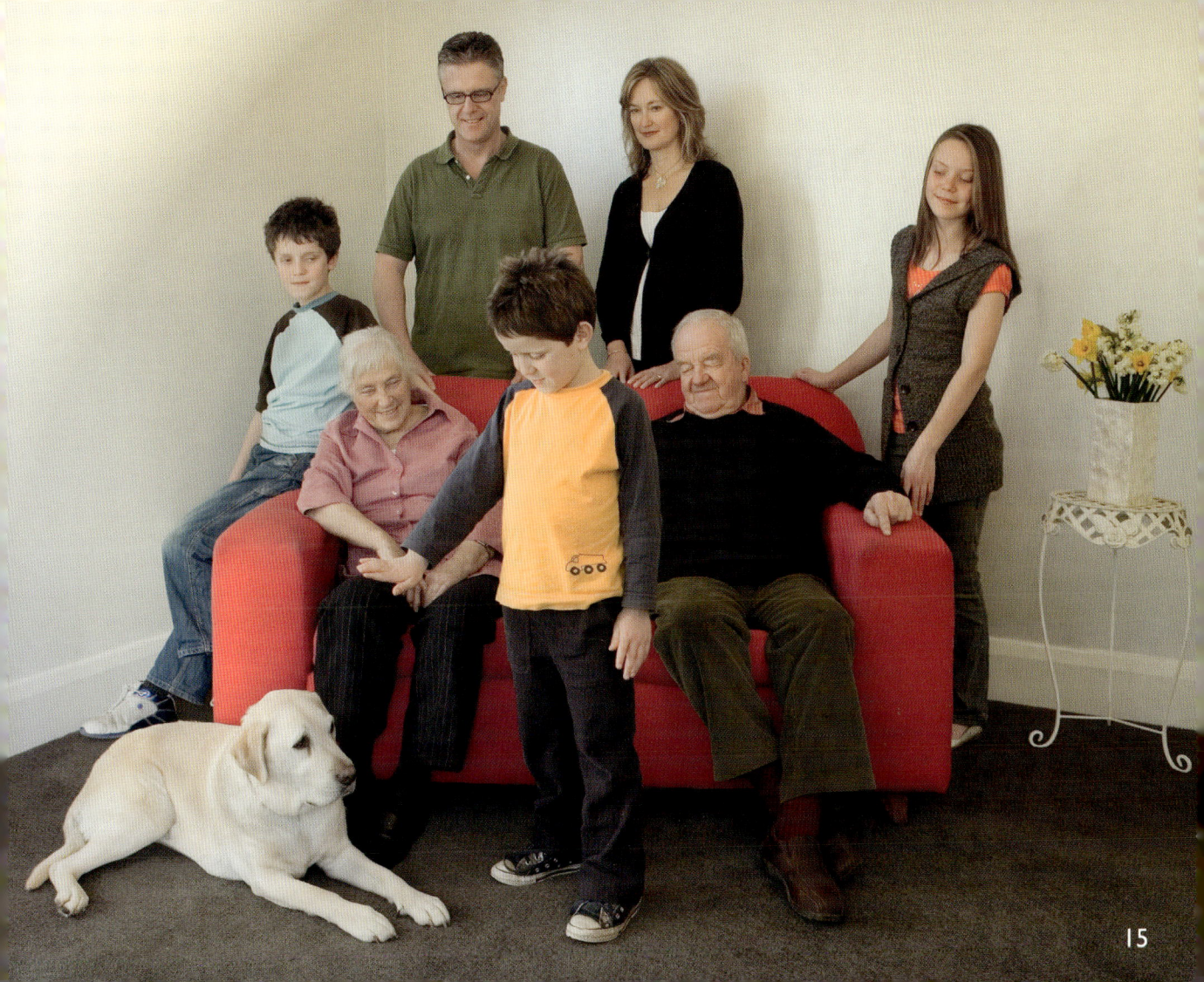

I go here.

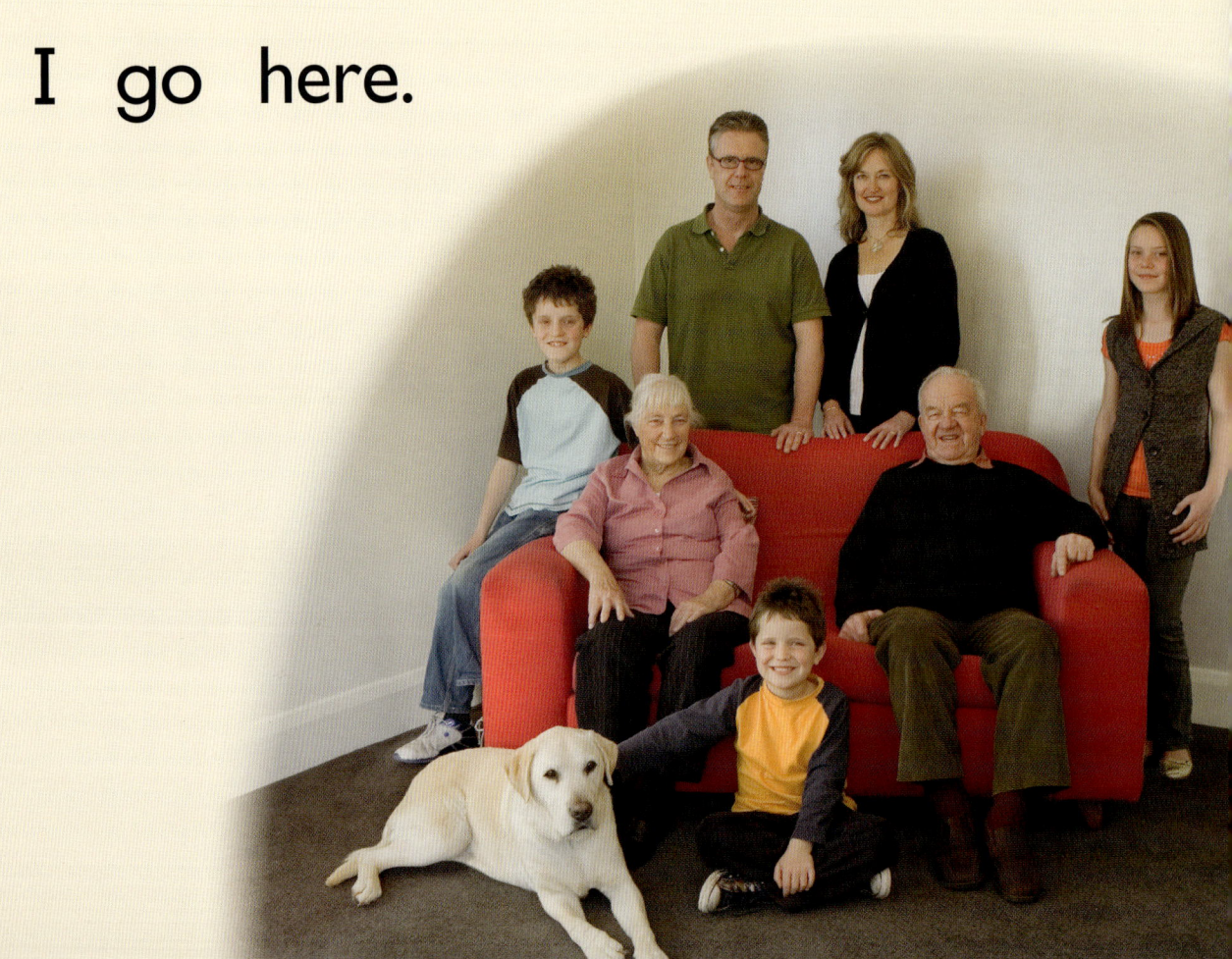